Seeking the Heart of God

Seeking the Heart of God

REFLECTIONS ON PRAYER

MOTHER TERESA
AND
BROTHER ROGER

HarperSanFrancisco

A Division of HarperCollins*Publishers*

PUBLISHED IN GREAT BRITAIN BY HARPERCOLLINS IN 1992;
FIRST U.S. EDITION PUBLISHED IN 1993

Library of Congress Cataloging-in-Publication Data

Teresa, Mother
    Seeking the heart of God : reflections on prayer /
Mother Teresa and Brother Roger.—1st U.S. ed.
      p. cm.
    Translated from the French.
    Originally published: London : Fount Paperbacks,
1992.
    ISBN 0–06–068238–8
    1. Prayer—Christianity—Meditations. I. Roger, frère.
II. Title.
BV210.2.T437 1993
248.3'2—dc20   92–54257

---

97 HAD 10 9 8 7 6 5 4

This edition is printed on acid-free paper that meets the
American National Standards Institute Z39.48 Standard.

Contents

Introduction

IN CALCUTTA, IN TAIZÉ, and in a host of other
places throughout the world, Mother Teresa and
Brother Roger meet men and women, many of
them young, who are athirst for God and who ask
them, "What is prayer?" and "How can we
pray?"

Young people today are often more interested
in persons than in ideas. They not only ask what
prayer means, they want to know how someone
is living it every day.

It is in response to these questions that Mother
Teresa and Brother Roger bring out this little
book now. In twelve chapters, each written half
by the one and half by the other, and based on
their own personal experience and the multitude
of encounters that make up their lives day after
day, they express what prayer is.

This conversation for two voices brings out at

the one time the deep similarities between them and the diversity of style. Their words are different, the language of fire is the same.

If this is now the third time that Mother Teresa and Brother Roger join forces to write a book, surely that is because they are drawn together by the profound intention of their lives: each in his or her own way has sought to respond to the great interrogations of the twentieth century through founding a community.

Overcome by the misery of the poorest of the poor, Mother Teresa began on her own in 1948 to provide a presence of love in a run-down neighbourhood of Calcutta. Today, her sisters can be found all over the world, coming to the help of those who are suffering physically and morally.

Refusing to accept passively the divisions of the Second World War, Brother Roger started in 1940 to create a community of men committed to the reconciliation of Christians and, through them, of the whole human family. He, too, was alone when he began. The very first people he welcomed were refugees, notably Jews. Today, with his brothers, he receives tens of thousands of young people from every continent who go to Taizé in a never ending pilgrimage.

Mother Teresa and Brother Roger met for the first time in August 1976, in Taizé. Mother

Teresa was on her way back from the USA, and Taizé was full of young people. To express what was in their hearts, they wrote a prayer together:

O God, Father of each human being, you ask everyone to bring love where the poor are humiliated, joy where the Church is demoralized, reconciliation where human beings are divided, fathers and sons, mothers and daughters, husbands and wives, believers and those who cannot believe, Christians and their unloved Christian brothers and sisters. You give us this way forward so that your Church, the torn apart Body of Jesus Christ, be a leaven of communion for the poor of the earth and in all the human family.

A few months later, Brother Roger was in Calcutta spending some time in a poor neighbourhood of the city, not far from Mother Teresa's house. Each day, he helped to care for abandoned children or for men close to death in the home for the dying. It was from Calcutta that Mother Teresa and Brother Roger together launched this appeal for reconciliation:

"We are both deeply questioned by the suffering in our contemporary world. In the face of the wounds of humanity, we find the divisions between Christians become unbearable. Shall we give up our separations and set ourselves free from our fear of one another? What is the use of trying to find out who was right and who was wrong? . . . O Christ, open all of us up to overcome ourselves: let us no longer put off reconciliation in that unique communion which is called the Church, irreplaceable yeast in the bread of humanity."

Mother Teresa went back to Taizé in 1983. In the midst of a crowd of young people, the two founders once again formulated what preoccupied them both:

"Both of us are conscious of the fact that great areas of the world are covered over by spiritual deserts. You can find young people in them who bear the marks of being abandoned by those closest to them and of a subtle form of doubt provoked by broken relationships which affect them to their very depths . . . Family breakdowns have wounded the innocence of their childhood or adolescence. What is the point of living? Does life still have any meaning? In Calcutta, there are homes for the dying that are visible for all to see, but in the West, many young people find themselves in real "homes for the dying" which the eye cannot see . . . And there are also elderly people who are obliged to end their days in isolation. And even if they have enough to subsist on materially, it is as if the only way out left to them is to wait for death to come."

Through the years, Mother Teresa and Brother Roger have met on a number of occasions, in different parts of the world. They both spoke, for example, during one of the prayers in the Coliseum, at the first world youth meeting, in 1984, in Rome.

The foundress of the Missionaries of Charity and the founder of Taizé are both witnesses for our time and the eyes of multitudes of young people on every continent look towards them. If you ask Mother Teresa or Brother Roger the secret of the love which has become compassion in them for every human creature, and first of all for the most abandoned, their response is identical: prayer is the source of a love that burns the heart.

ELIZABETH MARCHAND

1

One with Christ

————

IN REALITY, there is only one true prayer, only one substantial prayer: Christ himself. There is only one voice which rises above the face of the earth: the voice of Christ. Prayer is oneness with Christ.

When times come when we can't pray, it is very simple: if Jesus is in my heart, let Him pray, let Him talk to His Father in the silence of my heart. Since I cannot speak, He will speak; since I cannot pray, He will pray.

That's why often we should say, "Jesus in my heart, I believe in your faithful love for me." When we have nothing to give — let us give Him that nothingness. Let us ask Jesus to pray in us, for no one knows the Father better than He. No one can pray better than Jesus, who sends us His Spirit to pray in us, for we do not know how to pray as we ought.

And if my heart is pure, if in my heart Jesus is

alive, if my heart is a tabernacle of the living God, Jesus and I are one. As St Paul has said, "I live — yet no longer I: Christ lives in me."

Christ prays in me, Christ works in me, Christ thinks in me, Christ looks through my eyes, Christ speaks through my words, Christ works with my hands, Christ walks with my feet, Christ loves with my heart. As St Paul's prayer was: "I belong to Christ and nothing will separate me from the love of Christ." It was that oneness, oneness with God in the Holy Spirit.

It is very important for us to have Christ live in us so that we can have His presence wherever we are. God loves us so much. He gave His Son, Jesus. Now He gives us His love and you must let Him have a free hand with you. Not giving up everything — that is not important — what is important is compassion and presence. And the more we allow Him to live his life in us, the more we grow in the likeness of Christ.

Prayer is nothing but that complete surrender, complete oneness with Christ. And this is what makes us contemplatives in the heart of the world; for we are twenty-four hours then in His presence: in the hungry, in the naked, in the homeless, in the unwanted, unloved, uncared for. For Jesus said, "Whatever you do to the least of my brethren, you do it to me."

Our Father, here I am, at your disposal, your
  child,
to use me to continue your loving the world,
by giving Jesus to me and through me,
to each other and to the world.
Let us pray for each other that we allow Jesus
  to love in us
and through us with the love with which His
  Father loves him.

MOTHER TERESA

1

Inner light
_____

IF YOU KNEW that God always comes to you . . .
What matters most is discovering that God loves
you, even if you think that you do not love God.

As the twentieth century draws to a close, a
luminous Gospel insight which had been hidden
for a long time under the dust of the ages has been
brought to light: for every human being, even if
they are not aware of it, the Risen Christ is
present, "united to every human being without
exception".

Christ is waiting to be welcomed by each
person. If you are not able to respond, He
respects your silence. When you welcome Him,
by the Holy Spirit He creates within you an
intimate communion with Himself.

In the wonder of a communion, He makes his
home in the very depths of your soul. His
presence is as clear as your own existence.

Could you have doubts about this? Are chasms of unbelief opening up within you? You are not unfaithful for all that. Doubts may simply be the other side of faith.

The Risen Christ, invisibly present, could speak in this way: "I know that you experience days of monotony and darkness. I am familiar with your trials and your poverty, yet you are filled to overflowing: filled by the living springs, the wellsprings of faith, hidden in your depths."

The astonishing presence of Jesus, the Risen Lord, creates in you a source of light. It remains lit even when everything is shrouded in darkness; it bursts suddenly into flame like a coal still glowing under the ashes.

Sometimes you say to yourself: the fire in me is going out. But you were not the one who lit that fire. Your faith does not create God, and your doubts cannot banish Him to nothingness.

Remember: the simple desire for God is already the beginning of faith. Leading to eternal life, the trust of faith has a beginning but will have no end . . .

And a communion with the Risen Christ commits you to living Christ for others. Struggle and contemplation join hands. A century after the death of Christ, a believer wrote these words: "The calling God has given to Christians is so beautiful that they cannot abandon it." Abandon what? Abandon their responsibility for others.

Where would we be today if women, men and also children had not arisen at times when humanity seemed to be heading for the worst?

They were attentive to a fine human hope and to an invisible presence. They found a way to go beyond personal conflicts and to cross the barriers separating nations, spiritual families and races. They sensed, rising up from the depths of the peoples of the earth, an aspiration to a fullness of joy and peace, but also the unfathomable distress of the innocent.

As for you, are you going to let yourself fall asleep in dull indifference? Will your lips and your heart become frozen in an attitude of "what's the use, we can't do anything, let things take their course"? Will you let yourself sink into discouragement like Elijah, that believer of times gone by, who, convinced that he could do nothing more for his people, collapsed under a tree to fall asleep and forget?

Or will you remain awake and take your place among those women, men and children who have decided to act?

Through a life of inner peace, sharing and solidarity, they speak to us, they help us go forward. They possess unexpected energies in order to take on responsibilities.

They know that faith enables us to resist the worst torments, the soul overflowing with hope and love. Faith allows us to leave behind the time of mistrust, the time of suspicion, to enter into a time of trust and reconciliation.

Quite often the humble of this earth, almost without resources, have prepared ways forward. They have managed to kindle the flame of a communion with Christ, and the flame of a human hope, even in the night of peoples.

Four hundred years after Christ, a believer named Augustine lived in North Africa. He had experienced misfortunes, the death of his loved ones. One day he was able to say to Christ: "Light of my heart, do not let my darkness speak to me." In his trials, Saint Augustine realized that the presence of the Risen Christ had never left him; it was light in the midst of his darkness.

Jesus, your light is shining within us,
let not my doubts and my darkness speak to me;
Jesus, your light is shining within us,
let my heart always welcome your love.

BROTHER ROGER

2

You are precious to me

———

EVERY SINGLE CHILD has, you and I have been created for greater things: to love and to be loved.

We know from the Scriptures when God speaks to the prophet, He says, "I have called you by name; you are mine; you are precious to me; I love you." That saying means that to God Himself we are precious; He loves us and He wants us to love Him in return.

"Behold, I have graven you upon the palm of my hand." That is what Jesus came on earth to do: to proclaim, to give us the Good News that God loves us, that we are precious to Him.

He loves me. And how does He love me? As He says, "Even if a mother can forget her child, I will not forget you. I hold you in the palm of my hand." I was meditating on this text and I said, "Millions and millions must be in His hand, and yet He can see me – right there in His hand! I must be a very small particle somewhere, but must be there because He says so."

It is wonderful to think that thought when we suffer, when we feel lonely, when we feel troubled. Remember you are there – and just at that time when you suffer most His eyes are on you, you are precious to Him.

We are precious to Him
That man dying in the street – precious to Him
that millionaire – precious to Him
that sinner – precious to Him
Because He loves us.

We need prayer to understand God's love for us. If we really mean to pray and want to pray we must be ready to do it now. These are only the first steps towards prayer but if we never make the first step with determination, we will not reach the last one: the presence of God.

MOTHER TERESA

2

Today I would like to enter your home

As WE WELCOME so many young people to our hill of Taizé throughout the year, it happens that my brothers and I question ourselves: why has God entrusted to us such a beautiful adventure of faith? Seeing week after week their faces, Mediterranean or Scandinavian, Portuguese or Slavic, African or Asian, we ask ourselves: what do we wish most for them?

Our wish is that they may discover in the Risen Christ a meaning for their life. We would like them to receive, in the common prayer, through the times of reflection, and in their searching at the wellsprings of faith, a kind of "shock of meaning". And to each one of them I would like to say:

Your eyes are astonished to discover, even in faraway lands, young people who have fallen prey to discouragement. But your eyes perceive especially multitudes of young people attentive to discern the meaning of their life. They dare to say to themselves: "Get going! Begin again! Leave discouragement behind! Leave hopelessness behind! Let your soul live!"

Where can this inner vitality be found? It comes to life when, in faith, in a leap of trust, you live intensely in the present moment, God's today.

This dynamism is never acquired once and for all. At every stage of life, from childhood to old age, it involves the risk of setting out on the road time and time again. Some 2,600 years ago, a believer wrote: "God's plans for you are plans of peace and not of misfortune; God wants to give you a future and a hope."

Living intensely each present day means letting Christ dwell within you. His words are so clear: "Today I would like to enter your home."

Who is He, this Christ who offers such vitality?

In order to make Himself understood by human beings, God found no better way than coming to earth as one of the poor, as a humble man. He came through Christ Jesus. God would still be far away if Christ did not allow Him to shine through clearly.

From the beginning, Christ was in God. Since the birth of humanity, He was a living Word. He came to earth to make the trusting of faith accessible. Risen from the dead, He makes his home within us; He dwells within us by the Holy Spirit. And we discover that Christ's love is expressed first and foremost by His forgiveness and His continual presence within us.

Jesus Christ, Love of all loving, you were always in me and I did not know it. You were there, and I kept on forgetting you. You were in my heart of hearts and I was looking elsewhere. Even when I remained far from you, you kept on waiting for me. And the day is coming when I can tell you: Risen Christ, you are my life: I belong to Christ, I am Christ's.

BROTHER ROGER

3

Joy is prayer

————

JOY IS PRAYER, the sign of our generosity, selflessness and close and continued union with God.

Joy is prayer; joy is strength; joy is love, a net
of love by which you can catch souls. God loves
a cheerful giver. He gives most who gives with
joy. The best way to show our gratitude to God
and people is to accept everything with joy. A
joyful heart is the normal result of a heart
burning with love.

Let us not use bombs and guns to overcome
the world. Let us use love and compassion.
Peace begins with a smile – smile five times a day
at someone you don't really want to smile at at
all – do it for peace. So let us radiate the peace of
God and so light His light and extinguish in the
world and in the hearts of all people all hatred
and love for power.

Suffering in itself is nothing: but suffering

shared with Christ's passion is a wonderful gift. Yes, a gift and a sign of His love, because this is how the Father proved that He loved the world — by giving His Son to die for us.

Suffering, if it is accepted together, borne together, is joy. Remember that the passion of Christ ends always in the joy of the resurrection of Christ, so when you feel in your own heart the suffering of Christ, remember the resurrection has to come — the joy of Easter has to dawn. Never let anything so fill you with sorrow as to make you forget the joy of the Risen Christ.

We all long for heaven where God is, but we have it in our power to be in heaven with Him right now, to be happy with Him this moment. But being happy with Him now means loving as He loves, helping as He helps, giving as He gives, serving as He serves, rescuing as He rescues.

Therefore, even if you write a letter for a blind man or you just go and sit and listen, or you take the mail for him, or you visit somebody or bring a flower to somebody . . . it is never too small, for this is our love of Christ in action.

Prayer is joy . . . Prayer is love . . . Prayer is peace . . . You cannot explain it; you must experience prayer. It is not impossible. God gives it for the asking. "Ask and you shall receive." The father knows what to give his children – how much more our heavenly Father knows!

Lord Jesus, make us realize
that it is only by frequent deaths of ourselves
and our self-centred desires
that we can come to live more fully;
for it is only by dying with you
that we can rise with you.

MOTHER TERESA

3

Let the simple heart rejoice!

FOR MANY YEARS now, some of my brothers have been living in Bangladesh, sharing the life of the most destitute. One of them wrote me: "Our life has been deeply affected by the cyclone and the floods. Some of our neighbours ask us: Why all these misfortunes? Have we sinned so much?"

Often in the human heart there dwells a secret fear: God is going to punish me. When she was five years old, my little goddaughter Marie-Sonaly came to me one day in tears. Her adopted mother was in the hospital and the little girl said to me, "My mummy is ill; it's my fault. I hugged her too hard." Where do these guilt feelings come from, already so early in life?

To think that God punishes human beings is one of the greatest obstacles to faith. When God is seen as a tyrannical judge, Saint John reminds us in letters of fire: "God is love. We are not the ones who loved God; God loved us. Let us love, because God loved us first."

That is where everything begins: letting yourself be loved by God. But it's not so simple . . . Why is it that some Christians find it so hard to believe that they are loved? They say to themselves: God loves others, but not me.

Human beings are sometimes severe. God, for His part, comes to clothe us in compassion. He weaves our life, like a beautiful garment, with the threads of His forgiveness. He buries our past in the heart of Christ and He had already taken care of our future.

God loves you before you love Him. You think you are not waiting for Him, and He is waiting for you. You say "I am not worthy" and He places on your finger the ring of the prodigal son. That is how the Gospel turns things upside down.

We are all prodigals! In the depths of your captivity, you turn towards God, and bitterness disappears from your face. God's forgiveness inspires your own singing. And the contemplation of God's forgiveness becomes a radiant kindness in the simple hearts that let themselves be led by the Spirit.

With Mother Teresa, one day we visited the leper hospital. I saw a leper raise his emaciated arms and begin to sing these words: "God has not inflicted a punishment on me; I praise Him because my illness has turned into a visit from God." In his affliction, that man also had the intuition that suffering does not come from God.

God is not the author of evil. But He has accepted a huge risk. He wanted us to be creators with Him. He wanted human beings not to be like passive robots, but free to decide personally on the direction their lives will take, free to love or not to love.

And Christ never stands by passively while someone suffers. Risen from the dead, He accompanies each person in their suffering to such an extent that there is a pain God suffers, a pain Christ suffers. And, in His name, He enables us to share the distress of those who are undergoing incomprehensible trials; He leads us to alleviate the misery of the innocent.

Although human distress does not come from God, afterwards some people discover that they have been purified by their trials. To understand this, it is necessary to have gained maturity and also to have crossed inner deserts. I would like to give an example.

In February 1991 I was in the Philippines for a gathering of young people that my brothers had been preparing for several months. I paid a visit to an elderly woman, Aurora Aquino. Many

years before, her son Benigno had spent seven
years in prison, then he was exiled. When he was
able to return to his country, he was assassinated
just as he was getting off the plane. At the time, I
had noticed a photograph of Aurora Aquino in a
newspaper. Her face was that of a mother filled
with compassion.

Conversing with Aurora Aquino, I discovered
that, at the age of 81, she had no bitterness in her
heart. She even spoke these surprising words:
trials purify us. I was not astonished to find in her
such great selflessness. She is one of those elderly
persons of whom we can say: for whoever knows
how to love, for whoever knows how to suffer,
life is filled with serene beauty.

Affected by the shock of some event, might you
be undergoing the great trial, that of a broken
relationship? Or again, despised and humiliated,
have your purest intentions been distorted?

Humble prayer comes to heal the secret wound
of the soul. And the mystery of human suffering is
transfigured. The Spirit of the living God breathes
upon what is destitute and fragile. In our wounds
He causes living water to spring up. Through
Him the valley of tears becomes a place of living
springs.

Let the simple heart rejoice! From peace of
heart a Gospel joy can spring up, spontaneously.

God of every human being, you set in us an irreplaceable gift; you offer each person the capacity to be a reflection of your presence. By the Holy Spirit, you have engraved the will of your love in each of us, not on tablets of stone, but in the depths of our soul. And, by the peace of our heart, you enable us to make life beautiful for those around us.

BROTHER ROGER

4

A very simple way

MY SECRET IS quite simple: I pray.

It was the apostles who asked Jesus, "Jesus, teach us how to pray," because they saw Him so often pray and they knew that He was talking to His Father. What those hours of prayer must have been we know only from that continual love of Jesus for His Father, "My Father!" And He taught His disciples a very simple way of talking to God Himself.

Prayer to be fruitful must come from the heart and must be able to touch the heart of God. See how Jesus taught His disciples to pray:

Call God your Father; praise and glorify His name: "Our Father who art in heaven, hallowed by thy name."

Do His will, ask for daily bread, spiritual and temporal: "Thy kingdom come. Thy will be done on earth, as it is in heaven. Give us this day our daily bread."

Ask for forgiveness of your own sins and that we may forgive others, and also for the grace to be delivered from evil which is in us and around us: "And forgive us our trespasses, as we forgive those who trespass against us. And lead us not into temptation, but deliver us from evil."

Perfect prayer does not consist in many words, but in the fervour of the desire which raised the heart of Jesus.

We have ups and downs and sickness and
    suffering
That is part of the cross.
Anyone who imitates Him to the full
must share in His passion also.
That is why we need prayer
that is why we need the Bread of Life
that is why we have adoration
that is why we do penance.

We complicate prayer as we complicate many things. It is to love Jesus with undivided love – for you, for me, for all of us. And that undivided love is put into action when we do as Jesus said, "Love as I have loved you."

Love is a fruit in season at all times, and within reach of every hand. Anyone may gather it and no limit is set.

Before Jesus came God was great in His majesty, great in His creation. And then when Jesus came He became one of us, because His Father loved the world so much that He gave us His Son. And Jesus loved His Father and He wanted us to learn to pray by loving one another as the Father has loved Him.

"I love you," He kept on saying, "as the Father loved you, love Him." And His love was the cross. His love was the Bread of Life. And He wants us to pray with a clean heart, with a simple heart, with a humble heart. "Unless you become little children you cannot learn to pray, you cannot enter heaven, you cannot see God." To become a little child means to be one with the Father, to love the Father, to be at peace with the Father, our Father.

> I have come to you, Jesus, to take your touch
>   before I begin my day
> Let your eyes rest upon my eyes for a while
> Let me take to my work the assurance of your
>   friendship
> Fill my mind to last through the desert of
>   noise

Let your blessed sunshine fill the peaks of my
   thoughts
And give me strength for those who need me.

MOTHER TERESA

4

A kind of inner voice

GOD DOES NOT require of us, in our praying, extraordinary feats or superhuman efforts. In Christian history, many believers have lived lives rooted in the wellsprings of faith through a prayer quite poor in words.

Do you feel at a loss when confronted with that reality of prayer which, at first, seems so far beyond you? That has been true since the beginning of the Church. The apostle Paul wrote, "We do not know how to pray . . ." And he added: ". . . but the Holy Spirit comes to help our weakness and prays within us." Your heart can scarcely imagine it, but His Spirit is constantly active within you.

You aspire to feel the presence of God and you have the impression that nothing is there. Seven hundred years ago, a Christian named Meister Eckhart wrote, "Turning to God . . . does not mean thinking continually about God. It would be impossible for human nature to always have God in our minds, and anyway it would not be the best thing. Human beings cannot be satisfied with a God in the mind. For in that case, when we stopped thinking about God, God too would vanish . . . God is beyond human thought. And the reality of God never disappears."

A simple prayer, like a soft sighing, like a child's prayer, keeps us alert. Has not God revealed to those who are little, to Christ's poor, what the powerful of this world have so much trouble understanding?

Some people need to pray with many words to express what is in their hearts. But is it not better to speak them when we are by ourselves? When they are spoken in front of others, will they not oblige the others to listen to what was meant to be kept for God alone?

When Paul, the apostle, invites us to "pray without ceasing", that does not only mean expressing something in words. There is so much more to prayer than that! Words are only a tiny part. Prayer finds many expressions, gestures like the sign of the cross, symbols like that of offering oneself: for example, at the end of Saint Luke's Gospel, when Christ goes away, the disciples bow down, their faces to the ground.

Gospel realities can penetrate you through simple chants, sung over and over again: 'Jesus, your light is shining within us; let my heart always welcome your love." When you work, when you rest, these realities keep echoing within you.

Sometimes prayer is an inner struggle, and sometimes it means surrendering one's whole being. At a given moment, it becomes simply resting in God in silence. That is perhaps one of the high points of prayer.

Christ Jesus, in us there arises a kind of inner voice, and that voice is already our prayer. Though our lips may keep silence, our heart listens and also speaks to you. We are sometimes surprised to realize that you are in us, in a mysterious presence. And you, Risen Christ, you say to each person: surrender yourself quite simply to the life of my Spirit in you; your little bit of faith is enough; I will never leave you, never.

BROTHER ROGER

5

God is the friend of silence

THE BEGINNING OF prayer is silence.

If we really want to pray we must first learn to listen, for in the silence of the heart God speaks. And to be able to see that silence, to be able to hear God we need a clean heart; for a clean heart can see God, can hear God, can listen to God; and then only from the fullness of our heart can we speak to God. But we cannot speak unless we have listened, unless we have made that connection with God in the silence of our heart.

Prayer is not meant to be a torture, not meant to make us feel uneasy, is not meant to trouble us. It is something to look forward to, to talk to my Father, to talk to Jesus, the one to whom I belong: body, soul, mind, heart. Therefore we shall take as a special point silence of mind, eyes, and tongue.

First there is the silence of the mind and of the

heart: our Lady "kept all these things in her heart". This silence brought her close to our Lord, so that she never had to regret anything. See what she did when St Joseph was troubled. One word from her would have cleared his mind; she did not say that word, and our Lord Himself worked the miracle to clear her name. Would that we could be so convinced of this necessity of silence! I think then the road to close union with God would become very clear.

Then we have the silence of the eyes which will always help us to see God. Our eyes are like two windows through which Christ or the world comes to our hearts. Often we need great courage to keep them closed. How often we say, "I wish I had not seen this thing", and yet we take so little trouble to overcome the desire to see everything.

Silence of the tongue will teach us so much: to speak to Christ, to be joyful when with others, and to have many things to say. Christ speaks to us through others and at meditation He speaks to us directly.

God is the friend of silence.

We need to find God and He cannot be found in noise and restlessness. See how nature, the trees, the flowers, the grass grow in perfect silence – see the stars, the moon and the sun, how they move in

41

silence. The more we receive in silent prayer, the more we can give in our active life.

Silence gives us a new outlook on everything. We need silence to be able to touch souls. The essential thing is not what we say but what God says to us and through us.

Jesus is always waiting for us in silence. In that silence He will listen to us, there He will speak to our soul, and there we will hear His voice. In silence we will find new energy and true unity. The energy of God will be ours to do all things well. The unity of our thoughts with His thoughts, the unity of our prayers with His prayers, the unity of our actions with His actions, of our life with His life.

MOTHER TERESA

5

Peace of heart

—————

IT IS NOT EASY, for human words to express to God what lies in the depths of our being. Some days we pray with almost nothing. Remaining close to Christ in utter simplicity is already praying. And silence is sometimes everything in prayer.

Will you be able to welcome the Risen Christ even in the dry and thirsty ground of your body and your spirit? And the tiny, even hidden, event of your waiting causes springs of living water to well up: goodness of heart, looking beyond present difficulties, and also that inner harmony created by the life of the Holy Spirit poured out in us.

Will you remain in the Risen Christ's presence, during those long periods of silence when at first you seem to be in a desert? This silence seems to be nothing at all. But there, courageous decisions come to fruition.

When you pray, it can happen that you ask Christ, "What do you expect of me?" The day will come when you realize that He expects a lot. He expects you to be, for others, a witness of the trusting of faith, a kind of reflection of His presence.

Don't worry if you know so little about praying. Foundering in worry has never been a Gospel path. "No one can add a single day to their life by worrying about it . . . I give you my peace . . . Do not let your heart be troubled and afraid."

Fears and anxieties are part of our human condition, immersed as we are in societies that are wounded and shaken. Every human being, every believer, journeys, creates and suffers in these societies, and can experience inner impulses of revolt, sometimes of hatred and of domination.

By His Holy Spirit, the Risen Christ transfigures all that is most disconcerting in you. He reaches what was out of reach. All forms of pessimism that you harbour about yourself melt away; you can do away with subjective impressions.

An imperceptible inner transformation, the transfiguration of your being, continues your whole life long. It makes each day God's own today. It is, already on this earth, the beginning of the resurrection, the dawning of a life that has no end.

Wonder of a love without beginning or end . . . You will be surprised to find yourself saying:

This Jesus, the Risen Lord, was in me, and yet I didn't feel anything. So often I looked for Him elsewhere. As long as I kept fleeing the living springs He had set in the hollow of my being, run as I might across the earth, far, very far, I was only going astray on paths that lead nowhere. A joy in God was impossible to find.

But the time came when I discovered that Christ had never left me. I still did not dare to speak to Him, yet He already had understood me, already He was speaking to me. Baptism had been the mark of an invisible presence. When the veil of worry lifted, the trusting of faith came and illuminated even my night.

Christ Jesus, in your Gospel you tell us: why worry . . . by worrying you can do nothing! And each day you allow us to discover, at the living springs of faith, peace of heart, so essential in order to follow you and to build us up within.

BROTHER ROGER

45

6

Among us for all time

HOLY COMMUNION, as the word itself implies, is the intimate union of Jesus and our soul and body. If we want to have life and have it more abundantly, we must live on the flesh of the Lord. In Holy Communion we find Christ under the appearance of bread. In our work we find Him under the appearance of flesh and blood. It is the same Christ.

See Jesus in the tabernacle; fix your eyes on Him who is the light; bring your hearts close to His divine Heart; ask Him to grant you the grace of knowing Him, the love of loving Him, the courage to serve Him. Seek Him fervently. Every moment of prayer, especially before our Lord in the tabernacle, is a sure positive gain.

Where will you get the joy of loving? – in the Eucharist, Holy Communion. Jesus has made Himself the Bread of Life to give us life. Night and day, He is there. In our communities, we pray before the Blessed Sacrament one hour every day. And from the time we started this prayer, our love for Jesus became more intimate, our love for each other more understanding, our love for the poor more compassionate.

Jesus made Himself the Bread of Life to make sure we understand what He is saying, to satisfy our hunger for Him, to satisfy our love for Him. Even that is not enough for Him, so He makes himself the hungry one so we can satisfy His hunger for our love. And by doing to the poor what we are doing, we are satisfying His hunger for our love.

MOTHER TERESA

6

Adorable presence

CHRIST OFFERS HIMSELF in the Eucharist, adorable presence, it is there for you who are destitute. It is received in a spirit of poverty and repentance of heart, with the soul of a child, until the very evening of your years.

"My Kingdom is within you": the Eucharist constantly brings to life these words of Christ, even when there is no apparent resonance, and even for someone who hardly dares imagine it.

In remaining before the Eucharist for long periods of time, many people have let themselves be penetrated down to the very depths of their being. For all who consent to a long process of maturation, little by little their inner self is built up, without their knowing how. And, by prayer that is always simple, they are somehow drawn towards Christ.

Who is He, this Christ, Love of all loving?

Could He be the one John the apostle refers to when he writes, "Someone you do not know is in your midst"?

He is the one who, risen from the dead, rejoices with us, today, tomorrow and always. In Him, the wellsprings of jubilation never run dry.

He is also the one who bears with us the great sorrows of life, the broken relationships. . . . In His life on earth, Jesus, fully human, was deeply affected in His heart of hearts by the trials of others. He wept when someone He loved died; He wept when his friend Lazarus died.

More accessible for one person, more hidden for another, we seem to hear Him say, "Don't you realize that I am close beside you and by the Holy Spirit I live in you? Don't be afraid. I am always with you, until the end of the world. I will never leave you. Never."

No matter how little we sense of the Holy Spirit, He is life for us. No matter how little we understand of the Gospel, it is light in our midst. No matter how little we grasp of the Eucharist, it is an adorable presence in us.

And when you were lingering far from Christ Jesus, He was already waiting for you with these Gospel words, "In you I have placed my joy."

Jesus, Risen Lord, you look at the heart, not at outward appearances. In the depths of our soul, sometimes we call you: Christ Jesus, I am not worthy of you, but only say a word and my soul will be calmed, healed. And you never create in us, Christ, either torment or anguish, but your continual presence comes to awaken the joy of living in you.

BROTHER ROGER

7

I look at Him and He looks at me

———

OFTEN A DEEP fervent look at Christ may make the most fervent prayer. "I look at Him and He looks at me" is the most perfect prayer.

Today when everything is questioned and changed let us go back to Nazareth. Jesus had come to redeem the world – to teach us that love of His Father. How strange that He should spend thirty years just doing nothing, wasting His time! Not giving a chance to His personality or to His gifts, for we know that at the age of twelve He silenced the learned priests of the temple who knew so much and so well. But when His parents found Him, He went down to Nazareth and was subject to them.

For thirty years we hear no more of Him – so that the people were astonished when He came in public to preach, He a carpenter's son, doing just the humble work in a carpenter's shop – for thirty years.

Through a life of contemplation we come to realize God's constant presence and His tender love for us in the least little things of life: to be constantly available to Him, loving Him with our whole heart, whole mind, whole soul and whole strength, no matter in what form He may come to us. Jesus comes in the bodies of our poor. They are there for the finding. Jesus comes to you and me and, very often, we pass Him by.

These two aspects of life, action and contemplation, instead of excluding each other, call for each other's help, implement and complete each other. Action, to be productive, has need of contemplation. The latter, when it gets to a certain degree of intensity, diffuses some of its excess on the first. By contemplation the soul draws directly from the heart of God the graces which the active life must distribute.

I think if we can spread this prayer, if we can translate it into our lives, it will make all the difference. It is so full of Jesus. It has made a great difference in the lives of the Missionaries of Charity:

Dear Jesus,
Help us to spread your fragrance everywhere
   we go.
Flood our souls with your Spirit and life

Penetrate and possess our whole being so
  utterly
that our lives may only be a radiance of yours.
Shine through us
and be so in us
that every soul we come in contact with
may feel your presence in our soul.
Let them look up and see no longer us
but only Jesus.
Stay with us
and then we shall begin to shine as you shine,
so to shine as to be light to others.
The light, O Jesus, will be all from you.
None of it will be ours.
It will be you shining on others through us.
Let us thus praise you in the way you love best
by shining on those around us.
Let us preach you without preaching
not by words, but by our example
by the catching force
the sympathetic influence of what we do
the evident fullness of the love our hearts bear
  to you.

MOTHER TERESA

7

A contemplative outlook

IN THE BEAUTY of a common prayer, a veil is lifted
on what, in faith, cannot be expressed in words,
and this reality beyond words evokes our adoration. A mystical outlook sees in it reflections of
heaven's joy on earth.

A contemplative outlook sets you free from
deadening routines. It allows you to perceive
Gospel treasures in the humblest events. It
discerns the presence of the Risen Christ even in
the most forsaken human beings. It discovers in
the universe the radiant beauties of creation.

In the image of God, humans are creators too.
A contemplative outlook enables us to admire
what human beings create with their own hands,
from childhood to death. There are artists' hands
whose creations permit us to discern Gospel
faces, so that just to look at them is enough for us
to catch sight of the mystery of God.

When we realize that God loved us first, even before we loved Him, then we are filled with astonishment. Contemplation is nothing else than the attitude whereby our whole being is totally seized by the wonder of a love.

Although in all of us there are wounds, there is above all in each person the mystery of a Presence.

Deep within each one of us there lies vast reaches of the unknown, of doubt, of secret distress, and also chasms of guilt which come from who knows where. But gradually we understand that, in the depths of the human person, Christ prays, more than we imagine. Let the Holy Spirit pray within us with the trust of a child, and we can then realize that these depths are inhabited.

And moments arise when God is everything.

Alongside you, Jesus the Christ, it becomes possible to know God, by letting our life be penetrated by the little we have understood of the Gospel. And this little is just enough for us to go forward, day after day. This is because you never make us into people who have arrived; we remain Christ's poor, our whole life long, people who, in all simplicity, dispose ourselves to place our trust in the Mystery of Faith.

BROTHER ROGER

8

Complete confidence

IF WE REALLY fully belong to God, then we must be at His disposal and we must trust in Him. We must never be preoccupied with the future. There is no reason to be so. God is there.

In our communities, there has not been one single day that we have refused somebody, that we did not have food, that we did not have a bed or something, and we deal with thousands of people. We have 53,000 lepers and yet never has one been sent away. Though we have no salaries, no income, no nothing; we receive freely and give freely. This has been such a beautiful gift of God.

Our dependence on Divine Providence is a firm and lively faith that God can and will help us. That He can is evident, because He is almighty; that He will is certain, because He promised it in so many passages of Holy Scripture and because He is infinitely faithful to all His promises.

Christ encourages us to have this confidence in these words: "Whatever you ask in prayer, believe that you have received it, and it will be yours." The apostle St Peter also commands us to throw all cares upon the Lord who provides for us. And why should God not care for us since He sent us His Son and with Him all hope? St Augustine says: "How can you doubt that God will give you good things since He vouchsafed to assume evil for you?"

This must give us confidence in the Providence of God who preserves even the birds and the flowers. Surely if God feeds the young ravens which cry to Him, if He nourishes the birds which neither sow nor reap nor gather into barns, if He robes the flowers of the field so beautifully, how much more will He care for human beings whom He has made in His own image and likeness and adopted as His children, if we only act as such, keep His commandments and have confidence in Him.

I don't want the work to become a business but to remain a work of love. I want us to have that complete confidence that God won't let us down. Take Him at His word and seek first the kingdom of heaven, and all else will be added on.

Lord, help us to see in your crucifixion and
    resurrection
an example of how to endure
and seemingly to die in the agony and conflict
    of daily life,
so that we may live more fully and creatively.
You accepted patiently and humbly
the rebuffs of human life,
as well as all the tortures of your crucifixion
    and passion.
Help us to accept the pains and conflicts
that come to us each day
as opportunities to grow and to become more
    like you.
Enable us to go through them patiently and
    bravely,
trusting that you will support us.

MOTHER TERESA

8

If a trusting heart were at the beginning of everything . . .

SOMETIMES YOU WONDER: where are the sources of an inner life? Happy those who go forward, not by sight, but by the trust of faith.

When, in your night, you go to these sources, the thirsting for trust brings light within. And you want to say to God, "Listen, listen to my child's prayer. Help me to entrust all things to you at every moment. I want to find my joy in your continual presence."

If everything began with a heart that trusts, who would continue to say: What am I doing on this earth?

It sometimes happens that the trust deep down within us is swept away by events that shake us. In the Gospel, Jesus assures us that we can do nothing by worrying. It is up to us to accept our limitations and the things that are fragile within us.

Why dwell on what hurts, both in ourselves and in others?

We know the words of one of the first witnesses to Christ: "Even if our hearts condemn us, God is greater than our hearts."

Jesus the Christ does not invite you to be preoccupied with yourself. But to a humble repentance of heart. What does that mean? It means that movement of trust whereby you cast your faults on Him. And there you are, released, even liberated, ready to live the present moment intensely, never discouraged because always forgiven.

Perhaps you say, "That's not possible"? When you feel unloved and not really understood, Christ Jesus keeps on telling you, "Do not be afraid, I am here. I love you with a love that will never end. Do you love me?" And you reply, "I love you, Jesus, perhaps not as I would like to, but I do love you."

Breath of Christ's loving, Holy Spirit, in each one of us you place faith; it is like a burst of trust repeated time and time again our whole life long, a simple trusting, so simple that all can welcome it.

BROTHER ROGER

61

9

A clean heart

─────

TO BE ABLE TO PRAY we need a pure heart. With a pure heart we can see God.

Prayer gives us a clean heart and that's the beginning of holiness. Holiness is not a luxury of the few; it is a simple duty for you and for me.

Where does holiness begin? In our own hearts. That's why we need that continual prayer – to keep our hearts clean, for the clean heart becomes the tabernacle of the living God.

Jesus has made Himself the Bread of Life to give us His life, so that we can become like Him. So let us be like Jesus, full of compassion, full of humility towards each other, for in loving one another we love Him. You and I have every opportunity to become very holy through prayer, sacrifice and love. Let us pray for each other that we may grow more and more in the likeness of Christ.

Jesus Christ has told us that we ought "always to pray and not to faint", that is, not to grow weary of doing so. St Paul says, "Pray without ceasing". God calls all men to this disposition of the heart, of praying always.

Let the love of God once and for all take entire and absolute possession of a heart; let it become to the heart like second nature; let that heart suffer nothing that is contrary to it; let it apply itself continually to increase this love of God by seeking to please Him in all things and refusing Him nothing that He asks; let it accept as from His hand everything that happens to it; let it have a firm determination never to commit any fault deliberately and knowingly or, if it should fall, to be humble for it and to rise up again at once. Such a heart will pray continually.

Knowledge of God gives love and knowledge of self gives humility. Humility is nothing but truth. What have we got that we have not received? asks St Paul. If I have received everything, what good have I of my own? If we are convinced of this, we will never raise our head in pride. If you are humble, nothing will touch you, neither praise nor disgrace, because you know what you are. If you are blamed you will not be discouraged. If they call you a saint you will not put yourself on a pedestal. Self-knowledge puts us on our knees.

Change your hearts . . .
Unless we change our hearts we are not converted.
Changing places is not the answer.
Changing occupations is not the answer.
The answer is to change our hearts.
And how do we change?
By praying.

MOTHER TERESA

9

God's joy in our human world

————

AT A VERY YOUNG AGE I was struck by words
written several centuries before Christ: "Praised
be the Lord and I am delivered from the
opponent!" The spirit of praise brings us out of
ourselves and lets us place in God what worries
and nags at us. And the resistances in our depths
are transfigured.

The spirit of praise comes to life when common
prayer transmits God's joy in our human world.

In the churches of Russia, the profundity of the
choral singing, the incense, the icons, little
windows opening on to the realities of the
Kingdom of God, everything calls us to discern
"heaven's joy on earth". Our being is caught up
in its entirety, not only the mind but the body as
well.

It is so essential that common prayer allow us
to glimpse the adorable presence of the Risen

Christ, in particular through the beauty of the singing and the hymns.

The violinist Yehudi Menuhin wrote: "As soon as words are sung, they penetrate to the very depths of our soul. I am convinced that the young people who keep away from the churches today would flock to them if they found the mystery that should be experienced there."

When a child takes turns singing a prayer with adults, he supports all the generations. His presence helps us see that God always creates something new in our lives. At Taizé, each day children take part in the community prayer. During the celebration they light an oil-lamp, a symbol of Christ who is light. And a child from our village sings a prayer.

It takes very little to make churches welcoming: small candles, some fabric, an old carpet. And it is a good idea to fix up another room where people can meet to talk and to share a little food.

Someone's home too can reveal a glimpse of the unseen by a few symbols recalling the presence of God, an icon before which a lamp is burning. . . . When societies become more secularized, a home can be a place where those who are welcomed are awakened to the wellsprings of faith.

In each baptized person the Holy Spirit sets a larger or smaller portion of a "pastoral" gift, to communicate to others a mystery of hope. The little we understand of the Gospel bears fruit in us when we share it with others, no matter how timidly.

At Taizé one question is constantly on our minds: are the young people we welcome aware enough of their inner resources in order to prepare the ways of the Lord in those God entrusts to them?

When, around 1957, young adults began coming to Taizé in greater numbers; we did not think that it would last and we gave them accommodation three kilometres away. But we quickly realized that hospitality according to the Gospel meant that we had to welcome them very close to us. Now young people come every week of the year. It is essential to welcome them with no ulterior motives. We have always refused to create a youth movement linked to Taizé. Our wish is for them to discover Christ in His communion, that unique communion which is the Church. To go forward, once they have returned home, it is a good idea for them to create small communities of five or six. But, so that there may be no segregation of ages, we suggest that these small communities of young

67

people be linked to the local Christian communities, parishes and congregations, where all
the generations are present, from the elderly to
little children.

Living God, by the spirit of praise, you draw us
out of ourselves and our hesitations. To us,
Christ's poor, you have entrusted a mystery of
hope and you enable us to communicate it
above all by the lives we live.

BROTHER ROGER

10

Give Jesus a home in our homes

————

Smike at one another. It is not always easy. Sometimes I find it hard to smile at my Sisters but then we must pray. We must give Jesus a home in our homes for only then can we give Him to others.

If you learn the art of being thoughtful, you will become more and more Christlike, for His heart was meek and He always thought of the needs of others. Jesus went about doing good. Our Lady did nothing else in Cana but thought of the needs of the others and made their needs known to Jesus.

Jesus taught us to learn from Him, to be meek and humble of heart. If we are meek and humble, we will love each other as He loves us.

All over the world, there is terrible hunger for love. So bring prayer into your family, bring it to your little children. Teach them to pray. For a child that prays is a happy child. A family that prays is a united family. And to stay together you must love one another as God loves you, and He loves you tenderly.

It is very important for children to hear their parents talk about God. The children must be able to ask about God.

Once I gave a prayer to a non-believer and he took it back to his family and the children started to pray. When he saw me again he said, "Mother, you don't know how your prayer and picture have disturbed the whole family. The children want to know who God is. They want to know why Mother is speaking this way."

Children watch: they will learn that it makes a difference how they live their lives by watching what the parents do.

We can say to God:

> My Lord I love you
> my God I am sorry
> my God I believe in you
> my God I trust you.
> Help us to love one another
> as you love us.

MOTHER TERESA

10

To the sources of reconciliation

ARE YOU AMONG THOSE who open up ways of
easing tensions and of bringing reconciliations?
Will you create paths of trust in the human
family, and still more in that unique communion
which is the Body of Christ, His Church? Prepare
yourself to welcome the gift of doing this. And the
gifts of the Holy Spirit will never run out.

When I started Taizé, more than fifty years ago,
I asked myself: why is it that so many Christians,
although they profess faith in Christ who is love,
remain separated and even' go to the point of
tearing apart that communion which is His
Church? Reconciliation among Christians is so
essential to make Christ visible to non-believers.
And so I said to myself: try the impossible – to
create a small community where each day a few
men will attempt to live lives of trust and
reconciliation.

Since the 1960s, my brothers and I have been coming and going in the countries of Eastern Europe. We have understood that, in the East as well as in the West, reconciled Christians can be an irreplaceable ferment for building up the European family as well as the entire human family across the earth.

Seeking reconcilation and trust involves an inner struggle. It does not mean taking the easy way out. Nothing vast, nothing lasting can be created by following the line of least resistance. The spirit of reconciliation is not naïve but it is a widening of the heart, a deep kindness; it does not listen to suspicions.

In the middle of this century, a man named John had a crystal-clear intuition concerning reconciliation between Christians. Announcing a council, John XXIII said in January 1959: "We will not put history on trial. We will not seek to find out who was wrong and who was right. We will say: let us be reconciled!"

Today, interest in the ecumenical vocation has changed. Illusory hopes have given rise to disappointment, to a retreat. This only makes clearer Christ's call to be reconciled "without delay", within one's own heart, to be reconciled out of love. Is there a clearer light than this call? Who would wish to trample on it?

Reconciliation is never lazy. For the Gospel, it is immediate. It does not waste its time imputing bad intentions to others. It is careful never to dramatize situations.

Even if we had the gift of speaking in God's name, even if we had enough faith to move mountains, if we have no love, it is useless.

Are you ready to love only those who love you? Anyone can do that, without needing the Gospel. Jesus the Christ calls us to love even those who hurt us, and to pray for them.

When we pray for them and nothing seems to happen, does that mean that our prayer is not being heard? No, unanswered prayer does not exist. When we entrust to God those who have clashed with us, something may indeed change within them, but our own heart is already on a road of peace.

When you are hurt and humiliated, will you go on forgiving till your very last ounce of strength? That is what loving to the end means.

Can there be no miracles on earth? Yet love which forgives is one.

When you forgive and come up against a refusal, the answer of the Gospel is clear: it invites you to forgive seventy times seven times – in other words always, even in the face of coldness and distance.

73

Is your forgiveness being taken advantage of? Do others reason in this way concerning you: "I can do anything I like and even break this person; he is a believer; in the end he will forgive me because of Christ and the Gospel"? Love that forgives is not blind; it is clear-sighted. But it even renounces having to know what the other person will do with the forgiveness.

When wounds of the past are reopened, will you forgive even those who are no longer on this earth?

Jesus Christ, inner Light, you came not to judge the world but so that, through you, the Risen Lord, every human being might be saved, reconciled. And when the love that forgives becomes a fire within us, then the heart, even when afflicted, can begin to love anew.

BROTHER ROGER

11

Christ in His Body, the Church

THERE IS ONLY ONE voice which rises above the face of the earth: the voice of Christ. That voice reunites and co-ordinates in itself all the voices raised in prayer. There are many who do not know how, many who do not dare, and many who do not want to pray. In the communion of saints we act and pray in their names.

We have to pray on behalf of those who do not pray. We should be professionals in prayer. The apostles understood this very well. When they saw that they might be lost in a multitude of works, they decided to give themselves to continual prayer and to the ministry of the Word.

We want so much to pray properly and then we fail. We get discouraged and give up on prayer. God allowed the failure but He did not want the discouragement. He wants us to be more child-like, more humble, more grateful in prayer, and not to try to pray alone, as we all belong to the mystical body of Christ, which is praying always. There is no such thing as "I pray", but Jesus in me and Jesus with me prays; therefore the Body of Christ prays.

Many young people want holiness, want the complete surrender of their lives to God. They are afraid to join Christians if they expect that total surrender to God and then don't find it. These difficulties are all over the world.

The Church of God needs saints today. This imposes a great responsibility on us. We must become holy, not because we want to feel holy, but because Christ must be able to live His life fully in us. We put our undivided love for Christ in action by fulfilling what the Church has entrusted to us.

In our communities we take a fourth vow of giving wholehearted and free service to the poorest of the poor.

The fruit of our work, the ability to do this work is from prayer. The work we do is the fruit of our union with Christ. For this we have been called: to give Jesus to the people in the world. That the people can look up and see His love, His compassion, His humility in action.

People throughout the world may look different, or have a different religion, education or

position, but they are all the same. They are all
people to be loved. They are all hungry for love.
The people you see in the streets of India or Hong
Kong are hungry in body, but the people in
London or New York have also a hunger which
must be satisfied. Every person needs to be loved.

God made us for greater things: to love and to
be loved. What matters is that we love. We
cannot love without prayer and so whatever
religion we are we must pray together.

MOTHER TERESA

11

Mystery of communion

YOU ASPIRE TO FOLLOW Christ and you are wondering: how can I discover the will of His love? Do you hear His voice echoing within you: Come, I will give you a place to rest your heart; come, follow me!

For those who wish to follow Christ, it can happen that, at first, the "yes" and the "no" wrestle within. One seems to contend with the other. Any choice means deciding from among various options and it is natural to want to have everything and not give up anything.

Why do you hesitate to commit yourself by saying "yes" for your whole life? Perhaps you think that in order to say yes to Christ, exceptional qualities are needed and that you do not have them.

Are we aware enough that all of us remain poor? We are Christ's poor. All of us can say: My

78

faith is weak, but the Holy Spirit is present; He will support me to the end; He will make it possible for me to live a beautiful and vast adventure of trust in God and will enable me to commit myself with the same yes with which the Virgin Mary said to God, "let it happen to me as you have said".

Does this "yes" include a portion of human error? Step by step, our whole life long, Christ comes to transfigure what will be born and reborn through him. And the Gospel call becomes clearer: there is no greater love than to give our life for those God entrusts to us.

You want to follow Christ, and so you will discover that you cannot stop halfway. Christ uses this suggestive image to speak to those who have committed themselves with him: whoever puts their hand to the plough cannot look back.

As you seek to follow Christ without putting it off until later, know that you are not alone; you live as part of the Church. By the Holy Spirit, the mysterious presence of the Risen Christ has become tangible in a visible communion, the Church. Gathering "women and men of all nations, he makes them mystically into his own Body".

Christ is communion. He did not come to start one more religion, but to offer a communion in

Himself. He wrests you away from isolation and consequently you can say to Him, "Jesus, my joy, my hope and my life, look not on my sins but on the faith of your Church. In the footsteps of the witnesses of all the ages, from Mary and the apostles down to believers of the present day, enable me day after day to dispose myself inwardly, to put my trust in the Mystery of Faith."

In that unique communion which is the Church, Christ offers you all you need to go to the wellsprings of trust – the Gospel, the Eucharist, the peace of forgiveness . . . and the holiness of Christ is no longer out of reach, it is quite close to you. It overflows especially in the unfailing goodness of a human heart, in a selfless love.

Without this mystery of communion which is the Church, how would the light of the Risen Christ have been transmitted across the ages, from Mary and the apostles until today?

And you, will you question yourself? How can you prepare the ways of the Lord Christ for others? In other words: how can you permit continuities of Christ in the Church and, through it, in the human family?

You have heard the "come, follow me" of Christ Jesus and, like the young man in the Gospel, after having hesitated you would like to respond by a "yes", committing your entire life.

This "yes" leaves you exposed, there is no other way.

You seek to follow Christ, so remember: light in your darkness, He loves you as if you were the only one: that is His secret.

Jesus, Risen Lord, you are the Saviour of every life, and so we would always like to remain alongside you. Keep us from ever abandoning you on the roadside. And when we discover our frailties, at that moment hidden resources are revealed in us – an inner strength, a dynamism that comes from you.

BROTHER ROGER

12

To serve the poor

————

CHARITY FOR THE POOR whom we love, because it
is in them that today we find Jesus, the Word
incarnate, is like a living flame. The more united
we are to God, the greater will be our love and
readiness to serve the poor wholeheartedly.
Much depends on this unison of hearts.

Don't search for God in far lands. He is close to
you. He is with you. Just keep the lamp burning
and you will always see Him. Watch and pray.
Keep kindling the lamp and you will see His love
and you will see how sweet is the Lord you love.

Jesus has offered His lifelong, faithful, personal friendship in tenderness and love to each
one of us. He has espoused us to Himself. So now
by our presence we put that love into action. Jesus
went about doing good. And we are trying to
imitate Him now because I believe that God loves
the world through us. I see so many people in the

street. People unwanted, unloved, uncared for, people hungry for love. They are Jesus. Where are you?

"I thirst", said Jesus on the cross. He spoke of His thirst not for water, but for love. He, the Creator of the universe, asked for the love of His creatures. He thirsts for our love. These words "I thirst," do they echo in our souls? Money is useful only if it serves to spread Christ's love. It can serve to feed the hungry Christ. But He is hungry not just for bread, but for love, for your presence, for your human contact.

To offer a home to the homeless Christ, we must start by making our own homes places where peace, happiness and love abound, through our love for each member of our family and for our neighbours. Once we have learned to love with a love that hurts, our eyes will open and we will be able to give that love. So let us be one heart full of love, full of joy, full of peace. Let us radiate that love, that joy and that peace by growing more and more in the likeness of Christ.

Let us remember that whatever we offer each other, whether it be a smile, or a piece of bread, or tender love, or a helping hand – Jesus will take all that as done to Him: "You did it to me." But let there be no pride or vanity in the work. The work is God's work; the poor are God's poor. Put yourself completely under the influence of Jesus, so that He may think His thoughts in your mind; do His work through your hands, for you will be all powerful with Him who strengthens you.

We know that what we are doing is just a drop in the ocean. But if that drop were not there, the ocean would be less because of that missing drop.

What matters is the individual. To get to love the person, we must come in close contact with him. I believe in person-to-person contact. Every person is Christ for me, and since there is only one Jesus, that person is the one person in the world at that moment.

Through my prayer I become one in love with Christ and see that praying to Him is loving Him, and that means fulfilling His words. The poor in the world's slums are like the suffering Christ. In them God's Son lives and dies and through them God shows me His true face. Prayer for me means being twenty-four hours a day at one with the will of Jesus, to live for Him, through Him and with Him.

And then, one day, we will go to meet Christ in heaven. Our Lord will show His gratitude and He will say, "Come! Come to me, you blessed of my Father, because I was hungry, you gave me to eat; I was naked, you clothed me; I was homeless, you took me in."

To serve the poor

Make us worthy, Lord
To serve our fellow-men
Throughout the world
Who live and die in poverty and hunger.
Give them, through our hands,
This day their daily bread;
And by our understanding love,
Give peace and joy.

MOTHER TERESA

12

Human solidarities

THE GOSPEL DOES NOT place us in the time of fear, but in the time of trust. It does not regard human beings with pessimism.

Happy all who discover, in the Risen Christ, a trust that will not pass away, that will not wear out. Far from running away from human solidarities, it leads us to live Christ for others and to take on responsibilities.

Because of Christ and the Gospel, who will seek to alleviate suffering in places where there is sickness or hunger or appalling housing conditions? Who could keep their eyes shut in the face of those who are oppressed, ill-treated, victims of clever manoeuvring? Where creation is wounded, who could remain indifferent?

In order to make the earth more welcoming and a better place to live, the vast possibilities of science and technology need to be put to use.

They are able to offer relief in misfortune, to bring an end to famines, to sustain, throughout the earth, the human family that is growing to unprecedented proportions.

Indispensable though they may be, these powerful means by themselves are not enough.

If we were to wake up one fine morning in societies that were functional, highly technological, but where the trust of faith, the intelligence of the heart and a thirst for reconciliation had been extinguished, what then would be the future of the human family?

Who will be attentive to the distress of the innocent: children scarred by broken families, elderly persons experiencing unbearable loneliness?

When children see their loved ones argue or separate, their hearts are wounded for life. It is not too much to say that broken relationships, human abandonment, are one of the worst traumas of the end of the twentieth century. If young people were to go to spend time with these children who suffer from broken relationships, they could listen to them, speak to them and perhaps bring them to a common prayer.

Some young people are overcome by doubt and are not able to trust in the living God, abandoned as they have been by those to whom God entrusted them from birth. A void has opened up in them, a deep pit that they are unable to fill. And now it is as if they wanted to run further and yet further to find a chance in life, a mother, a father.

When their heart is dying, when their depths cry out in loneliness, when from deep within them there wells up the ultimate question: but where is God? then who will remind them that, for God, "every human being is sacred, yes consecrated, by the wounded innocence of their childhood"?

And there are so many elderly people who are all alone. Sometimes they think that they have been nothing, accomplished nothing. And yet, so many elderly persons are able to listen without being judgemental, to understand the searching of those younger than them. They are often found in churches. Why not go and join them there? They have made possible the continuities of Christ in the human family. Who will kiss their worn hands to express gratitude?

Speaking of human solidarities, I would like to say a few words about my brothers. Since the beginning of our community, we have been led to stand firm at the heart of the human family's situations, with all their constant ebb and flow. We ask ourselves: how to understand, without letting ourselves be carried away by the successive waves? And we have grasped the fact that human solidarities need to be nourished at the sources of faith, in an inner life.

When I see some of my brothers giving their lives for those entrusted to them, at Taizé or in the harsh conditions of destitute neighbourhoods around the world, I say to myself: forgetting oneself, selflessness, is one of the burning breaths of the Gospel.

We have chosen the way of a great simplicity. Our vocation has committed us to living solely from our work, accepting neither donations nor bequests nor gifts – nothing, absolutely nothing. For decades now, welcoming as we do young people, from the West and now from the East too, what have we discovered? With a minimum of material resources, we are enabled to accomplish a welcome that at first seemed unachievable.

*　　*　　*

On all the continents, so many young people, women, men and also children, have all they need for the healing of wounded situations. Will you, too, be among them?

A young man from Estonia who had come to Taizé said: "If we have become believers, and if we are here in Taizé, it's thanks to our grandmothers, and we would have liked to have brought them to Taizé with us. Most of our grandmothers were deported for many years — fifteen years, seventeen years. Out there, during their deportation, in order to keep going, all they had was trust in God. They are simple women. They could not understand why there was so much suffering, why their homes were destroyed, their children and husbands killed. Some came back from the camps in Siberia; they are transparent and have no bitterness. For us now, our grandmothers are saints.''

For trust to grow in the world, in the East and in the West, in the North or in the South, your life and the lives of a great many people are necessary. The experience of a whole lifetime is not necessary in order to begin.

During these years, some have risen up and, with their bare hands, have brought down walls of fears and humiliations. They knew that no one people is more guilty than another. It is so essential never to humiliate members of a nation some of whose leaders, in the course of history, have committed acts of terror.

There are multitudes of people who have given the best of themselves to be a leaven of trust among individuals and peoples. They have risen up among human beings as signs of what we never dared hope for. They have been built up within by times of incomprehensible trial. They have persevered, come what may. So many of them have, by their lives, shone without knowing it with the holiness of Christ.

Will you, too, come to the point of giving yourself in this way? Will you hear the words that Jesus, the Christ, addresses to each person, "You, follow me"?

Perhaps you are saying: I don't have the courage. Then remember this call: leave discouragement behind, leave hopelessness behind, let your soul live! Yes, in the name of Christ, let your soul live!

Christ Jesus, you want nobody to experience inner distress. And you come to illuminate in us the profound mystery of human suffering. By it, we come close to an intimacy with God. Holy Spirit, Comforter, make us able to alleviate the pain of the innocent and to be attentive to those whose lives, placed in situations of trial, are radiant with the holiness of Jesus the Christ.

BROTHER ROGER

Mother Teresa of Calcutta

MOTHER TERESA founded the Missionaries of Charity, a congregation of sisters in Calcutta which has rapidly spread to all continents. They devote themselves to the service of the poorest of the poor, both materially and spiritually.

Mother Teresa (Agnes Ganxhe Bojaxhiu) was born in Skopje, Yugoslavia, of Albanian parents, in 1910. At eighteen, convinced that she was called to be a missionary, she entered a congregation of sisters working in India. While teaching in a high school in Calcutta, she became more and more concerned at the dire needs of the people living in the nearby slums, and gradually she came to realize that her place was "in the midst of the poorest of the poor, the least of Christ's brothers and sisters".

In 1948, dressed in a simple cotton sari, she went to live with the poor in the streets of the city, intending to start a congregation to care for them. She began by opening a small school in a slum. She wrote the letters of the Bengali alphabet in the mud with a stick in order to teach her pupils to read and write.

At that time, a great many incurably ill people were left to die in the streets because the overcrowded hospitals could not keep them. Their great distress led Mother Teresa to open her first Home for the Dying in 1954. Hindus, Muslims and Christians were welcomed without distinction, and could die with dignity and respect for their beliefs.

Little by little, the sisters of Mother Teresa grew in number. She called them "missionaries of charity". In addition to the three vows of poverty, chastity and obedience, they make a fourth commitment, that of "giving wholehearted and free service to the poorest of the poor".

Wherever they are, the sisters try to assist Christ suffering in the most destitute: those who are hungry and thirsty, naked and home-less, orphans, the sick and dying, prisoners, the handicapped, lepers, as well as alcoholics and drug addicts, those who are grieving or unloved, those who have become a burden to society or who have lost all confidence in life.

Living also in rich countries, Mother Teresa and her sisters have discovered that spiritual poverty – loneliness, lack of love – are deep problems, sometimes more difficult to solve than material poverty.

Brother Roger of Taizé

BROTHER ROGER founded the Taizé Community as an attempt to open ways of healing the divisions between Christians and, through the reconciliation of Christians, to overcome conflicts in the human family.

Everything began in solitude when, in August 1940, at the age of twenty-five, he left his home country, Switzerland, to go and live in France, his mother's birthplace. For several years he had already been reflecting on the possibility of creating a community where it would be possible actually to live out reconciliation day after day. He wanted to do this in a place where war and human distress were rife. While the Second World War was raging, he settled in the tiny village of Taizé, in Burgundy, a short distance from the line of demarcation that divided France in half. He offered hiding to political refugees, notably Jews.

Little by little other brothers joined him and, in 1949, the small community made life-commitments: celibacy, accepting the ministry of the prior, community of material and spiritual goods. The first brothers were from Protestant backgrounds, but soon Catholic brothers also joined them and today there are brothers from some twenty different nations.

The Community accepts no gifts or donations for its daily life, not even any personal inheritances that the brothers might have. They earn their living and share with others solely by their own work.

Beginning in the 1950s, some brothers went to live in disadvantaged places of the world, to be witnesses of peace, to live alongside those who suffer. Today, brothers live in small groups in destitute areas of Asia, Africa, North and South America. They attempt to share the living conditions of those around them. Brother Roger himself spends time regularly in places of poverty across the world. Beginning in 1962, with great discretion, brothers and young people sent from Taizé made many visits to Eastern European countries, to be close to those who were trapped within their frontiers.

From 1957 onwards, young adults began coming to Taizé in greater numbers. From

Portugal or Sweden, from Scotland or Poland, then from other continents, they take part in week-long meetings bringing together young people from thirty-five to seventy different nationalities. Some weeks, there are as many as six thousand there. Over the years, hundreds of thousands of young adults have passed through Taizé to reflect on a basic theme: inner life and human solidarity. At the wellsprings of the faith, they attempt to find a meaning for their life; they prepare themselves to take on responsibilities in the places in which they live.

Since 1966, the Sisters of St Andrew, an international Catholic community founded 750 years ago, have been living in a neighbouring village; they help with the work of welcoming people to Taizé.

To give support to the young, Taizé started a "pilgrimage of trust on earth". This pilgrimage does not organize participants into a movement centred on the Community but stimulates them to be creators of peace, bearers of reconciliation, in their home towns and villages, and in their local churches, involving all generations, from the elderly to little children. As a stage in this pilgrimage, at the end of each year a six-day European meeting brings together several tens of thousands of young adults in one city in Eastern or Western Europe. They are offered hospitality by the parishes of the city. The meeting in Prague, at the end of 1990, brought together 80,000 young people from all over Europe.

Today, everywhere in the world, the name of Taizé evokes a longing for a springtime of the Church, a Church that is, beyond present difficulties, a land of sharing and communion, a ferment of reconciliation at the heart of humanity.